For families of Angel babies.
May a rainbow appear, and their
memory never fade. — AJM

This edition published in 2024.

McDonald, Antoinette.
      Where's Baby, Momma? / written by Antoinette McDonald
      p. cm.
      Summary: A family experiences a pregnancy loss and through the understanding of God's love, the family shares the news with their toddler daughter.
      ISBN 979-8-218-97174-8

One day, Mom and Dad sat Moneek down to share some great news.

"Honey, we love you so much," said Mom.
"We know that you've wanted someone to play with,"
Dad said with a huge smile.

Mom and Dad grabbed Moneek closer, each holding her hand.
Dad began, "Mom and me love you more than life itself."

Mom looked deeper in her eyes, "We are going to have a baby."
Moneek stared in amazement and began to dance around the room.

"A baby? For us? Yeah!" Moneek danced to the rhythm of her own drum.

Mom and Dad sat entwined watching their only child dance around, with tears in their eyes. They prayed.

Moneek was quiet, head down looking at her shoes.
"What will the baby call me?"
Mom and Dad looked at each other, smiled and said, "Sissy!"
Moneek really liked it.

The months flew past – February and then March. Mom and Dad went to the doctor and found out that the baby is a little girl. They were so excited. They prayed.

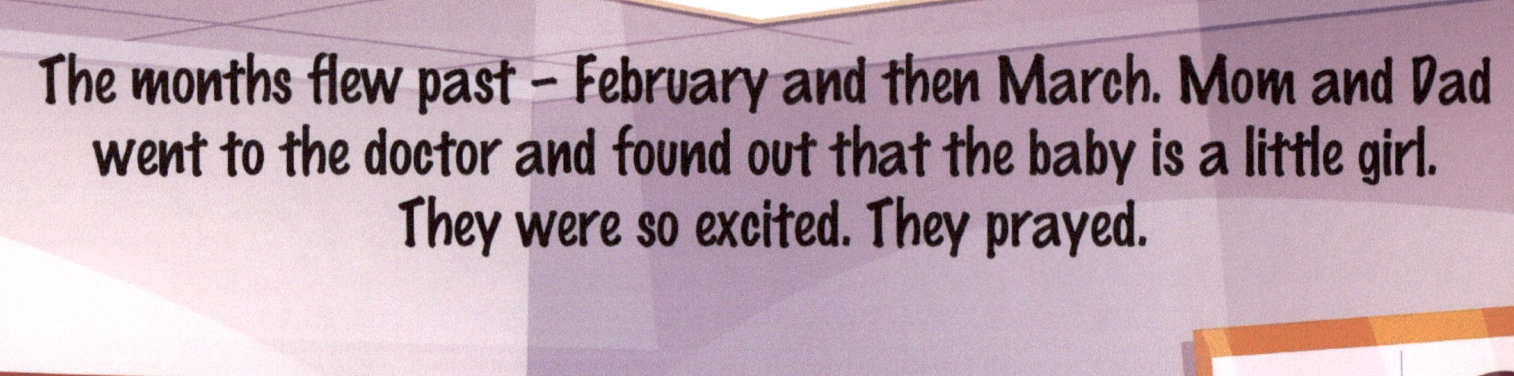

Since Mom and Dad shared the great news,
Mom's belly continued growing...

Growing, and GROWING!!!

Mom and Dad went to the doctor's in May.
They found out that the baby was not growing in Mommy's tummy.
They prayed.

Every day, Mom kissed Moneek goodbye in the morning and greeted her after school, all while in the bed.

One Sunday, while cuddled together Mom began to cry.
They all prayed.

Mom and Dad went to the hospital and stayed the night. All night they prayed.

They named the baby, Nia A'Joi. Nia is Swahili for 'purpose'.
Her life had a purpose although they didn't
know it, at that moment.

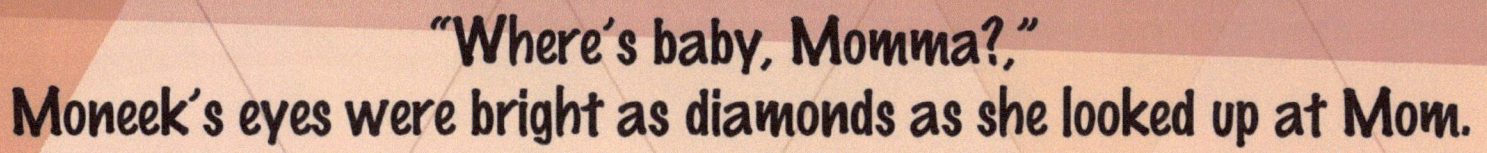

"Where's baby, Momma?,"
Moneek's eyes were bright as diamonds as she looked up at Mom.

LOVE
YOURSELF

Mom explained that Nia went to sleep, in mommy's tummy and didn't wake up. That Moneek's sister went to heaven to be with God.

Moneek was sad and began to cry, so did Mom and Dad.
They all cried. They prayed.

Since Moneek was three years old, Mom and Dad explained it in a way that was easy for Moneek to understand.

"Nia was sick and couldn't get better! God called for her to come to heaven with Him!," Mom began to cry.

Dad continued, "We held Nia and prayed over her. We know God will love her and keep her until we see her again."

Moneek smiled. "Ok, she is safe with God! I love you!"
Mom, Dad and Moneek hugged each other. They prayed.